The Rise Of The Dutch Republic

Volume 7

by

John Lothrop Motley

Double9 BOOKS

The Rise Of The Dutch Republic
Volume 7
by John Lothrop Motley

ISBN: 978-93-75551-51-5

Published by

DOUBLE 9 BOOKS
2/13-B, Ansari Road
Daryaganj, New Delhi – 110002
info@double9books.com
www.double9books.com
Tel. 011-40042856

ABOUT THE AUTHOR

John Lothrop Motley was an American historian and diplomat renowned for his detailed studies on the political and social evolution of the Netherlands. Born in Dorchester, Massachusetts, to Thomas Motley and Ann Lothrop Motley, he developed a deep interest in European history and diplomacy that would define his intellectual pursuits. Educated at prestigious institutions, he later embarked on a career that combined scholarship and public service, producing some of the most significant historical works of his time. His best-known writings include The Rise of the Dutch Republic and The History of the United Netherlands, which vividly depict the Netherlands' struggle for independence and political identity. Motley's historical approach blended meticulous research with a literary narrative style that captured the moral and emotional dimensions of history. Alongside his literary achievements, he served as a diplomat, representing the United States abroad with distinction. His legacy endures as that of a historian who united rigorous scholarship with eloquent expression and human insight.

CONTENTS

1561-1562 [CHAPTER III]

The great cause of the revolt which, within a few years, was to break forth throughout the Netherlands; was the inquisition. It is almost puerile to look further or deeper, when such a source of convulsion lies at the very outset of any investigation. During the war there had been, for reasons already indicated, an occasional pause in the religious persecution. Philip had now returned to Spain, having arranged, with great precision, a comprehensive scheme for exterminating that religious belief which was already accepted by a very large portion of his Netherland Subjects. From afar there rose upon the provinces the prophetic vision of a coming evil still more terrible than any which had yet oppressed them. As across the bright plains of Sicily, when the sun is rising, the vast pyramidal shadow of Mount Etna is definitely and visibly projected—the phantom of that ever-present enemy, which holds fire and devastation in its bosom—so, in the morning hour of Philip's reign, the shadow of the inquisition was cast from afar across those warm and smiling provinces—a spectre menacing fiercer flames and wider desolation than those which mere physical agencies could ever compass.

There has been a good deal of somewhat superfluous discussion concerning the different kinds of inquisition. The distinction drawn between the papal, the episcopal, and the Spanish inquisitions, did not, in the sixteenth century, convince many unsophisticated minds of the merits of the establishment in any of its shapes. However classified or entitled, it was a machine for inquiring into a man's thoughts, and for burning him if the result was not satisfactory.

The Spanish inquisition, strictly so called, that is to say, the modern or later institution established by Pope Alexander the Sixth and Ferdinand the Catholic, was doubtless invested with a more complete apparatus for inflicting human misery, and for appalling human imagination, than any of the other less artfully arranged inquisitions, whether papal or episcopal. It had been originally devised for Jews or Moors, whom the Christianity of the age did not regard as human beings, but who could not be banished without depopulating certain districts. It was soon, however, extended from pagans to heretics. The Dominican Torquemada was the first Moloch to be placed upon this pedestal of blood and fire, and from that day forward the "holy office" was almost exclusively in the hands of that band of brothers. In the eighteen years of Torquemada's administration; ten thousand two hundred and twenty individuals were burned alive, and ninety-seven thousand three hundred and twenty-one punished with infamy, confiscation of property, or perpetual imprisonment, so that the total number of families destroyed by this one friar alone amounted to one hundred and fourteen thousand four hundred and one. In course of time the jurisdiction of the office was extended. It taught the savages of India and America to shudder at the name of Christianity. The fear of its introduction froze the earlier heretics of Italy, France, and Ger many into orthodoxy. It was a court owning allegiance to no temporal authority, superior to all other tribunals. It was a bench of monks without appeal, having its familiars in every house, diving into the secrets of every fireside, judging, and executing its horrible decrees without responsibility. It condemned not deeds, but thoughts. It affected to descend into individual conscience, and to punish the crimes which it pretended to discover. Its process was reduced to a horrible simplicity. It arrested on suspicion, tortured till confession, and then punished by fire. Two witnesses, and those to separate facts, were sufficient to consign the victim to a loathsome dungeon. Here he was sparingly supplied with food, forbidden to speak, or even to sing to which pastime it could hardly be thought he would feel much inclination—and then left to himself, till famine and misery should break his spirit. When that time was supposed to have arrived he was examined. Did he confess, and forswear his heresy, whether actually innocent or not, he might then assume the sacred shirt, and escape with confiscation of all his property. Did he persist in the avowal of his innocence, two witnesses sent him to the stake, one witness to the rack. He was informed of the testimony against him, but never confronted with the witness. That accuser might be his son, father, or the wife of his bosom, for all were enjoined, under the death penalty, to inform the inquisitors of every suspicious word which might fall from their nearest relatives. The indictment being thus supported, the prisoner was tried by torture. The rack was the court of justice; the criminal's only advocate was his fortitude—for the nominal counsellor, who was permitted no communication with the prisoner, and was furnished neither with documents nor with power to procure evidence, was a puppet, aggravating the lawlessness of the proceedings by the mockery of legal forms: The torture took place at midnight, in a gloomy dungeon, dimly, lighted by torches. The victim—whether man, matron, or tender virgin—was stripped naked, and stretched upon the wooden bench. Water, weights, fires, pulleys, screws—all the apparatus by which the sinews could be strained without cracking, the bones crushed without breaking, and the body racked exquisitely without giving up its ghost, was now put into operation. The executioner, enveloped in a black robe from head to foot, with his eyes glaring at his victim through holes cut in the hood which muffled his face, practised successively all the forms of torture which the devilish ingenuity of the monks had invented. The imagination sickens when striving to keep pace with these dreadful realities. Those who wish to indulge their curiosity concerning the details of the system, may easily satisfy themselves at the present day. The flood of light which has been poured upon the subject more than justifies the horror and the rebellion of the Netherlanders.

The period during which torture might be inflicted from day to day was unlimited in duration. It could only be terminated by confession; so that the scaffold was the sole refuge from the rack. Individuals have borne the torture and the dungeon fifteen years, and have been burned at the stake at last.

Execution followed confession, but the number of condemned prisoners was allowed to accumulate, that a multitude of victims might grace each great gala-day. The auto-da fe was a solemn festival. The monarch, the high functionaries of the land, the reverend clergy, the populace regarded it as an inspiring and delightful recreation. When the appointed morning arrived, the victim was taken from his dungeon. He was then attired in a yellow robe without sleeves, like a herald's coat, embroidered all over with black figures of devils. A large conical paper mitre was placed upon his head, upon which was represented a human being in the midst of flames, surrounded by imps. His tongue was then painfully gagged, so that he could neither open nor shut his mouth. After he was thus accoutred, and just as he was leaving his cell, a breakfast, consisting of every delicacy, was placed before him, and he was urged, with ironical politeness, to satisfy his hunger. He was then led forth into the public square. The procession was formed with great pomp. It was headed by the little school children, who were immediately followed by the band of prisoners, each attired in the horrible yet ludicrous manner described. Then came the magistrates and nobility, the prelates and other dignitaries of the Church: the holy inquisitors, with their officials and familiars, followed, all on horseback, with the blood-red flag of the "sacred office" waving above them, blazoned upon either side with the portraits of Alexander and of Ferdinand, the pair of brothers who had established the institution. After the procession came the rabble. When all had reached the neighborhood of the scaffold, and had been arranged in order, a sermon was preached to the assembled multitude. It was filled with laudations of the inquisition, and with blasphemous revilings against the condemned prisoners. Then the sentences were read to the individual victims. Then the clergy chanted the fifty-first psalm, the whole vast throng uniting in one tremendous miserere. If a priest happened to be among the culprits, he was now stripped of the canonicals which he had hitherto worn; while his hands, lips, and shaven crown were scraped with a bit of glass, by which process the oil of his consecration was supposed to be removed. He was then thrown into the common herd. Those of the prisoners who were reconciled, and those whose execution was not yet appointed, were now separated from the others. The rest were compelled to mount a scaffold, where the executioner stood ready to conduct them to the fire. The inquisitors then delivered them into his hands, with an ironical request that he would deal with them tenderly, and without blood-letting or injury. Those who remained steadfast to the last were then burned at the stake; they who in the last extremity renounced their faith were strangled before being thrown into the flames. Such was the Spanish inquisition—technically—so called: It was, according' to the biographer of Philip the Second, a "heavenly remedy, a guardian angel of Paradise, a lions' den in which Daniel and other just men could sustain no injury, but in which perverse sinners were torn to pieces." It was a tribunal superior to all human law, without appeal, and certainly owing no allegiance to the powers of earth or heaven. No rank, high or humble, was safe from its jurisdiction. The royal family were not sacred, nor, the pauper's hovel. Even death afforded no protection. The holy office invaded the prince in his palace and the beggar in his shroud. The corpses of dead heretics were mutilated and burned. The inquisitors preyed upon carcases and rifled graves. A gorgeous festival of the holy office had, as we have seen, welcomed Philip to his native land. The news of these tremendous autos-da fe, in which so many illustrious victims had been sacrificed before their sovereign's eyes, had reached the Netherlands almost simultaneously with the bulls creating the new bishoprics in the provinces. It was not likely that the measure would be rendered more palatable by this intelligence of the royal amusements.

The Spanish inquisition had never flourished in any soil but that of the peninsula. It is possible that the King and Granvelle were sincere in their protestations of entertaining no intention of introducing it into the Netherlands, although the protestations of such men are entitled to but little weight. The truth was, that the inquisition existed already in the provinces. It was the main object of the government to confirm and extend the institution. The episcopal inquisition, as we have already seen, had been enlarged by the enormous increase in the number of bishops, each of whom was to be head inquisitor in his diocese, with two special inquisitors under him. With this apparatus and with the edicts, as already described, it might seem that enough had already been done for the suppression of heresy. But more had been done. A regular papal inquisition also existed in the Netherlands. This establishment, like the edicts, was the gift of Charles the Fifth. A word of introduction is here again necessary—nor let the reader deem that too much time is devoted to this painful subject. On the contrary, no definite idea can be formed as to the character of the Netherland revolt without a thorough understanding of this great cause—the religious persecution in which the country had lived, breathed, and had its being, for half a century, and in which, had the rebellion not broken out at last, the population must have been either exterminated or entirely embruted. The few years which are immediately to occupy us in the present and succeeding chapter, present the country in a daily increasing ferment from the action of causes which had existed long before, but which received an additional stimulus as the policy of the new reign developed itself.

Previously to the accession of Charles V., it can not be said that an inquisition had ever been established in the provinces. Isolated instances to the contrary, adduced by the canonists who gave their advice to Margaret of Parma, rather proved the absence than the existence of the system. In the reign of Philip the Good, the vicar of the inquisitor- general gave sentence against some heretics, who were burned in Lille (1448). In 1459, Pierre Troussart, a Jacobin monk, condemned many Waldenses, together with some leading citizens of Artois, accused of sorcery and heresy. He did this, however, as inquisitor for the Bishop of Arras, so that it was an act of episcopal, and not papal inquisition. In general, when inquisitors were wanted in the provinces, it was necessary to borrow them from France or Germany. The exigencies of persecution making a domestic staff desirable, Charles the Fifth, in the year 1522, applied to his ancient tutor, whom he had placed on the papal throne.

Charles had, however, already, in the previous year appointed Francis Van der Hulst to be inquisitor-general for the Netherlands. This man, whom Erasmus called a "wonderful enemy to learning," was also provided with a coadjutor, Nicholas of Egmond by name, a Carmelite monk, who was characterized by the same authority as "a madman armed with a sword." The inquisitor-general received full powers to cite, arrest, imprison, torture heretics without observing the ordinary forms of law, and to cause his sentences to be executed without appeal. He was, however, in pronouncing definite judgments, to take the advice of Laurens, president of the grand council of Mechlin, a coarse, cruel and ignorant man, who "hated learning with a more than deadly hatred," and who might certainly be relied upon to sustain the severest judgments which the inquisitor might fulminate. Adrian; accordingly, commissioned Van der Hulst to be universal and general inquisitor for all the Netherlands. At the same time it was expressly stated that his functions were not to supersede those exercised by the bishops as inquisitors in their own sees. Thus the papal inquisition was established in the provinces. Van der Hulst, a person of infamous character, was not the man to render the institution less odious than it was by its nature. Before he had fulfilled his duties two years, however, he was degraded from his office by the Emperor for having forged a document. In 1525, Buedens, Houseau and Coppin were confirmed by Clement the Seventh as inquisitors in the room of Van der Hulst. In 1531, Ruard Tapper and Michael Drutius were appointed by Paul the Third, on the decease of Coppin, the other two remaining in office. The powers of the papal inquisitors had been gradually extended, and they were, by 1545, not only entirely independent of the episcopal inquisition, but had acquired right of jurisdiction over bishops and archbishops, whom they were empowered to arrest and imprison. They had also received and exercised the privilege of appointing delegates, or sub-inquisitors, on their own authority. Much of the work was, indeed, performed by these officials, the most notorious of whom were Barbier, De Monte, Titelmann, Fabry, Campo de Zon, and Stryen. In 1545, and again in 1550, a stringent set of instructions were drawn up by the Emperor for the guidance of these papal inquisitors. A glance at their context shows that the establishment was not intended to be an empty form.

They were empowered to inquire, proceed against, and chastise all heretics, all persons suspected of heresy, and their protectors. Accompanied by a notary, they were to collect written information concerning every person in the provinces, "infected or vehemently suspected." They were authorized to summon all subjects of his Majesty, whatever their rank, quality, or station, and to compel them to give evidence, or to communicate suspicions. They were to punish all who pertinaciously refused such depositions with death. The Emperor commanded his presidents, judges, sheriffs, and all other judicial and executive officers to render all "assistance to the inquisitors and their familiars in their holy and pious inquisition, whenever required so to do," on pain of being punished as encouragers of heresy, that is to say, with death. Whenever the inquisitors should be satisfied as to the heresy of any individual, they were to order his arrest and detention by the judge of the place, or by others arbitrarily to be selected by them. The judges or persons thus chosen, were enjoined to fulfil the order, on pain of being punished as protectors of heresy, that is to say, with death, by sword or fire. If the prisoner were an ecclesiastic, the inquisitor was to deal summarily with the case "without noise or form in the process—selecting an imperial councillor to render the sentence of absolution or condemnation." If the prisoner were a lay person, the inquisitor was to order his punishment, according to the edicts, by the council of the province. In case of lay persons suspected but not convicted of heresy, the inquisitor was to proceed to their chastisement, "with the advice of a counsellor or some other expert." In conclusion, the Emperor ordered the "inquisitors to make it known that they were not doing their own work, but that of Christ, and to persuade all persons of this fact." This clause of their instructions seemed difficult of accomplishment, for no reasonable person could doubt that Christ, had he re-appeared in human form, would have been instantly crucified again, or burned alive in any place within the dominions of Charles or Philip. The blasphemy with which the name of Jesus was used by such men to sanctify all these nameless horrors, is certainly not the least of their crimes.

In addition to these instructions, a special edict had been issued on the 26th April, 1550, according to which all judicial officers, at the requisition of the inquisitors, were to render them all assistance in the execution of their office, by arresting and detaining all persons suspected of heresy, according to the instructions issued to said inquisitors; and this, notwithstanding any privileges or charters to the contrary. In short, the inquisitors were not subject to the civil authority, but the civil authority to them. The imperial edict empowered them "to chastise, degrade, denounce, and deliver over heretics to the secular judges for punishment; to make use of gaols, and to make arrests, without ordinary warrant, but merely with notice given to a single counselor, who was obliged to give sentence according to their desire, without application to the ordinary judge."

These instructions to the inquisitors had been renewed and confirmed by Philip, in the very first month of his reign (28th Nov. 1555). As in the case of the edicts, it had been thought desirable by Granvelle to make use of the supposed magic of the Emperor's name to hallow the whole machinery of persecution. The action of the system during the greater part of the imperial period had been terrible. Suffered for a time to languish during the French war, it had lately been renewed with additional vigor. Among all the inquisitors, the name of Peter Titelmann was now pre-eminent. He executed his infamous functions throughout Flanders, Douay, and Tournay, the most thriving and populous portions of the Netherlands, with a swiftness, precision, and even with a jocularity which hardly seemed human. There was a kind of grim humor about the man. The woman who, according to Lear's fool, was wont to thrust her live eels into the hot paste, "rapping them o' the coxcombs with a stick and crying reproachfully, Wantons, lie down!" had the spirit of a true inquisitor. Even so dealt Titelmann with his heretics writhing on the rack or in the flames. Cotemporary chronicles give a picture of him as of some grotesque yet terrible goblin, careering through the country by night or day, alone, on horseback, smiting the trembling peasants on the head with a great club, spreading dismay far and wide, dragging suspected persons from their firesides or their beds, and thrusting them into dungeons, arresting, torturing, strangling, burning, with hardly the shadow of warrant, information, or process.

The secular sheriff, familiarly called Red-Rod, from the color of his wand of office, meeting this inquisitor Titelmann one day upon the high road, thus wonderingly addressed him—"How can you venture to go about alone, or at most with an attendant or two, arresting people on every side, while I dare not attempt to execute my office, except at the head of a strong force, armed in proof; and then only at the peril of my life?"

"Ah! Red-Rod," answered Peter, jocosely, "you deal with bad people. I have nothing to fear, for I seize only the innocent and virtuous, who make no resistance, and let themselves be taken like lambs."

"Mighty well," said the other; "but if you arrest all the good people and I all the bad, 'tis difficult to say who in the world is to escape chastisement." The reply of the inquisitor has not been recorded, but there is no doubt that he proceeded like a strong man to run his day's course.

He was the most active of all the agents in the religious persecution at the epoch of which we are now treating, but he had been inquisitor for many years. The martyrology of the provinces reeks with his murders. He burned men for idle words or suspected thoughts; he rarely waited, according to his frank confession, for deeds. Hearing once that a certain schoolmaster, named Geleyn de Muler, of Audenarde, "was addicted to reading the Bible," he summoned the culprit before him and accused him of heresy. The schoolmaster claimed, if he were guilty of any crime, to be tried before the judges of his town. "You are my prisoner," said Titelmann, "and are to answer me and none other." The inquisitor proceeded accordingly to catechize him, and soon satisfied himself of the schoolmaster's heresy. He commanded him to make immediate recantation. The schoolmaster refused. "Do you not love your wife and children?" asked the demoniac Titelmann. "God knows," answered the heretic, "that if the whole world were of gold, and my own, I would give it all only to have them with me, even had I to live on bread and water and in bondage." "You have then," answered the inquisitor, "only to renounce the error of your opinions."—" Neither for wife, children, nor all the world, can I renounce my God and religious truth," answered the prisoner. Thereupon Titelmann sentenced him to the stake. He was strangled and then thrown into the flames.

At about the same-time, Thomas Calberg, tapestry weaver, of Tournay, within the jurisdiction of this same inquisitor, was convicted of having copied some hymns from a book printed in Geneva. He was burned alive. Another man, whose name has perished, was hacked to death with seven blows of a rusty sword, in presence of his wife, who was so horror- stricken that she died on the spot before her husband. His crime, to be sure, was anabaptism, the most deadly offence in the calendar. In the same year, one Walter Kapell was burned at the stake for heretical opinions. He was a man of some property, and beloved by the poor people of Dixmuyde, in Flanders, where he resided, for his many charities. A poor idiot, who had been often fed by his bounty, called out to the inquisitor's subalterns, as they bound his patron to the stake, "ye are bloody murderers; that man has done no wrong; but has given me bread to eat." With these words, he cast himself headlong into the flames to perish with his protector, but was with difficulty rescued by the officers. A day or two afterwards, he made his way to the stake, where the half-burnt skeleton of Walter Kapell still remained, took the body upon his shoulders, and carried it through the streets to the house of the chief burgomaster, where several other magistrates happened then to be in session. Forcing his way into their presence, he laid his burthen at their feet, crying, "There, murderers! ye have eaten his flesh, now eat his bones!" It has not been recorded whether Titelmann sent him to keep company with his friend in the next world. The fate of so obscure a victim could hardly find room on the crowded pages of the Netherland martyrdom.

This kind of work, which went on daily, did not increase the love of the people for the inquisition or the edicts. It terrified many, but it inspired more with that noble resistance to oppression, particularly to religious oppression, which is the sublimest instinct of human nature. Men confronted the terrible inquisitors with a courage equal to their cruelty: At Tournay, one of the chief cities of Titelmann's district, and almost before his eyes, one Bertrand le Blas, a velvet manufacturer, committed what was held an almost incredible crime. Having begged his wife and children to pray for a blessing upon what he was about to undertake, he went on Christmas-day to the Cathedral of Tournay and stationed himself near the altar. Having awaited the moment in which the priest held on high the consecrated host, Le Blas then forced his way through the crowd, snatched the wafer from the hands of the astonished ecclesiastic, and broke it into bits, crying aloud, as he did so, "Misguided men, do ye take this thing to be Jesus Christ, your Lord and Saviour?" With these words, he threw the fragments on the ground and trampled them with his feet.

> [Histoire des Martyrs, f. 356, exev.; apud Brandt, i. 171,172. It may be well supposed that this would be regarded as a crime of almost inconceivable magnitude. It was death even to refuse to kneel in the streets when the wafer was carried by. Thus, for example, a poor huckster, named Simon, at Bergen-op-Zoom, who neglected to prostrate himself before his booth at the passage of the host, was

> immediately burned. Instances of the same punishment for that offence might be multiplied. In this particular case, it is recorded that the sheriff who was present at the execution was so much affected by the courage and fervor of the simple-minded victim, that he went home, took to his bed, became delirious, crying constantly, Ah, Simon! Simon! and died miserably, "notwithstanding all that the monks could do to console him."]

The amazement and horror were so universal at such an appalling offence, that not a finger was raised to arrest the criminal. Priests and congregation were alike paralyzed, so that he would have found no difficulty in making his escape. Ho did not stir, however; he had come to the church determined to execute what he considered a sacred duty, and to abide the consequences. After a time, he was apprehended. The inquisitor demanded if he repented of what he had done. He protested, on the contrary, that he gloried in the deed, and that he would die a hundred deaths to rescue from such daily profanation the name of his Redeemer, Christ. He was then put thrice to the torture, that he might be forced to reveal his accomplices. It did not seem in human power for one man to accomplish such a deed of darkness without confederates. Bertrand had none, however, and could denounce none. A frantic sentence was then devised as a feeble punishment for so much wickedness. He was dragged on a hurdle, with his mouth closed with an iron gag, to the market-place. Here his right hand and foot were burned and twisted off between two red-hot irons. His tongue was then torn out by the roots, and because he still endeavored to call upon the name of God, the iron gag was again applied. With his arms and legs fastened together behind his back, he was then hooked by the middle of his body to an iron chain, and made to swing to and fro over a slow fire till he was entirely roasted. His life lasted almost to the end of these ingenious tortures, but his fortitude lasted as long as his life.

In the next year, Titelmann caused one Robert Ogier, of Ryssel, in Flanders, to be arrested, together with his wife and two sons. Their crime consisted in not going to mass, and in practising private worship at home. They confessed the offence, for they protested that they could not endure to see the profanation of their Saviour's name in the idolatrous sacraments. They were asked what rites they practised in their own house. One of the sons, a mere boy, answered, "We fall on our knees, and pray to God that he may enlighten our hearts, and forgive our sins. We pray for our sovereign, that his reign may be prosperous, and his life peaceful. We also pray for the magistrates and others in authority, that God may protect and preserve them all." The boy's simple eloquence drew tears even from the eyes of some of his judges; for the inquisitor had placed the case before the civil tribunal. The father and eldest son were, however, condemned to the flames. "Oh God!" prayed the youth at the stake, "Eternal Father, accept the sacrifice of our lives, in the name of thy beloved Son."—"Thou liest, scoundrel!" fiercely interrupted a monk, who was lighting the fire; "God is not your father; ye are the devil's children." As the flames rose about them, the boy cried out once more, "Look, my father, all heaven is opening, and I see ten hundred thousand angels rejoicing over us. Let us be glad, for we are dying for the truth."—" Thou liest! thou liest !" again screamed the monk; "all hell is opening, and you see ten thousand devils thrusting you into eternal fire." Eight days afterwards, the wife of Ogier and his other son were burned; so that there was an end of that family.

Such are a few isolated specimens of the manner of proceeding in a single district of the Netherlands. The inquisitor Titelmann certainly deserved his terrible reputation. Men called him Saul the persecutor, and it was well known that he had been originally tainted with the heresy which he had, for so many years, been furiously chastising. At the epoch which now engages our attention, he felt stimulated by the avowed policy of the government to fresh exertions, by which all his previous achievements should be cast into the shade. In one day he broke into a house in Ryssel, seized John de Swarte, his wife and four children, together with two newly-married couples, and two other persons, convicted them of reading the Bible, and of praying in their own doors, and had them all immediately burned.

Are these things related merely to excite superfluous horror? Are the sufferings of these obscure Christians beneath the dignity of history? Is it not better to deal with murder and oppression in the abstract, without entering into trivial details? The answer is, that these things are the history of the Netherlands at this epoch; that these hideous details furnish the causes of that immense movement, out of which a great republic was born and an ancient tyranny destroyed; and that Cardinal Granvelle was ridiculous when he asserted that the people would not open their mouths if the seigniors did not make such a noise. Because the great lords "owed their very souls"—because convulsions might help to pay their debts, and furnish forth their masquerades and banquets— because the Prince of Orange was ambitious, and Egmont jealous of the Cardinal—therefore superficial writers found it quite natural that the country should be disturbed, although that "vile and mischievous animal, the people," might have no objection to a continuance of the system which had been at work so long. On the contrary, it was exactly because the movement was a popular and a religious movement that it will always retain its place among the most important events of history. Dignified documents, state papers, solemn treaties, are often of no more value than the lambskin on which they are engrossed. Ten thousand nameless victims, in the cause of religious and civil freedom, may build up great states and alter the aspect of whole continents.

The nobles, no doubt, were conspicuous, and it was well for the cause of the right that, as in the early hours of English liberty, the crown and mitre were opposed by the baron's sword and shield. Had all the seigniors made common cause with Philip and Granvelle, instead of setting their breasts against the inquisition, the cause of truth and liberty would have been still more desperate. Nevertheless they were directed and controlled, under Providence, by humbler, but more powerful agencies than their own. The nobles were but the gilded hands on the outside of the dial—the hour to strike was determined by the obscure but weighty movements within.

Nor is it, perhaps, always better to rely upon abstract phraseology, to produce a necessary impression. Upon some minds, declamation concerning liberty of conscience and religious tyranny makes but a vague impression, while an effect may be produced upon them, for example by a dry, concrete, cynical entry in an account book, such as the following, taken at hazard from the register of municipal expenses at Tournay, during the years with which we are now occupied:

> To Mr. Jacques Barra, executioner, for having tortured, twice, Jean de Lannoy, ten sous.
>
> "To the same, for having executed, by fire, said Lannoy, sixty sous.
> "For having thrown his cinders into the river, eight sous."

This was the treatment to which thousands, and tens of thousands, had been subjected in the provinces. Men, women, and children were burned, and their "cinders" thrown away, for idle words against Rome, spoken years before, for praying alone in their closets, for not kneeling to a wafer when they met it in the streets, for thoughts to which they had never given utterance, but which, on inquiry, they were too honest to deny. Certainly with this work going on year after year in every city in the Netherlands, and now set into renewed and vigorous action by a man who wore a crown only that he might the better torture his fellow- creatures, it was time that the very stones in the streets should be moved to mutiny.

Thus it may be seen of how much value were the protestations of Philip and of Granvelle, on which much stress has latterly been laid, that it was not their intention to introduce the Spanish inquisition. With the edicts and the Netherland inquisition, such as we have described them, the step was hardly necessary.

In fact, the main difference between the two institutions consisted in the greater efficiency of the Spanish in discovering such of its victims as were disposed to deny their faith. Devised originally for more timorous and less conscientious infidels who were often disposed to skulk in obscure places and to renounce without really abandoning their errors, it was provided with a set of venomous familiars who glided through every chamber and coiled themselves at every fireside. The secret details of each household in the realm being therefore known to the holy office and to the monarch, no infidel or heretic could escape discovery. This invisible machinery was less requisite for the Netherlands. There was comparatively little difficulty in ferreting out the "vermin"—to use the expression of a Walloon historian of that age—so that it was only necessary to maintain in good working order the apparatus for destroying the noxious creatures when unearthed. The heretics of the provinces assembled at each other's houses to practise those rites described in such simple language by Baldwin Ogier, and denounced under such horrible penalties by the edicts. The inquisitorial system of Spain was hardly necessary for men who had but little prudence in concealing, and no inclination to disavow their creed. "It is quite a laughable matter," wrote Granvelle, who occasionally took a comic view of the inquisition, "that the King should send us depositions made in Spain by which we are to hunt for heretics here, as if we did not know of thousands already. Would that I had as many doubloons of annual income," he added, "as there are public and professed heretics in the provinces." No doubt the inquisition was in such eyes a most desirable establishment. "To speak without passion," says the Walloon, "the inquisition well administered is a laudable institution, and not less necessary than all the other offices of spirituality and temporality belonging both to the bishops and to the commissioners of the Roman see." The papal and episcopal establishments, in co-operation with the edicts, were enough, if thoroughly exercised and completely extended. The edicts alone were sufficient. "The edicts and the inquisition are one and the same thing," said the Prince of Orange. The circumstance, that the civil authorities were not as entirely superseded by the Netherland, as by the Spanish system, was rather a difference of form than of fact. We have seen that the secular officers of justice were at the command of the inquisitors. Sheriff, gaoler, judge, and hangman, were all required, under the most terrible penalties, to do their bidding. The reader knows what the edicts were. He knows also the instructions to the corps of papal inquisitors, delivered by Charles and Philip: He knows that Philip, both in person and by letter, had done his utmost to sharpen those instructions, during the latter portion of his sojourn in the Netherlands. Fourteen new bishops, each with two special inquisitors under him, had also been appointed to carry out the great work to which the sovereign had consecrated his existence. The manner in which the hunters of heretics performed their office has been exemplified by slightly sketching the career of a single one of the sub-inquisitors, Peter Titelmann. The monarch and his minister scarcely needed, therefore, to transplant the peninsular exotic. Why should they do so? Philip, who did not often say a great deal in a few words, once expressed the whole truth of the matter in a single sentence: "Wherefore introduce the Spanish inquisition?" said he; "the inquisition of the Netherlands is much more pitiless than that of Spain."

Such was the system of religious persecution commenced by Charles, and perfected by Philip. The King could not claim the merit of the invention, which justly belonged to the Emperor. At the same time, his responsibility for the unutterable woe caused by the continuance of the scheme is not a jot diminished. There was a time when the whole system had fallen into comparative desuetude. It was utterly abhorrent to the institutions and the manners of the Netherlanders. Even a great number of the Catholics in the provinces were averse to it. Many of the leading grandees, every one of whom was Catholic were foremost in denouncing its continuance. In short, the inquisition had been partially endured, but never accepted. Moreover, it had never been introduced into Luxemburg or Groningen. In Gelderland it had been prohibited by the treaty through which that province had been annexed to the emperor's dominions, and it had been uniformly and successfully resisted in Brabant. Therefore, although Philip, taking the artful advice of Granvelle, had sheltered himself under the Emperor's name by re-enacting, word for word, his decrees, and re-issuing his instructions, he can not be allowed any such protection at the bar of history. Such a defence for crimes so enormous is worse than futile. In truth, both father and son recognized instinctively the intimate connexion between ideas of religious and of civil freedom. "The authority of God and the supremacy of his Majesty" was the formula used with perpetual iteration to sanction the constant recourse to scaffold and funeral pile. Philip, bigoted in religion, and fanatical in his creed of the absolute power of kings, identified himself willingly with the Deity, that he might more easily punish crimes against his own sacred person. Granvelle carefully sustained him in these convictions, and fed his suspicions as to the motives of those who opposed his measures. The minister constantly represented the great seigniors as influenced by ambition and pride. They had only disapproved of the new bishoprics, he insinuated, because they were angry that his Majesty should dare to do anything without their concurrence, and because their own influence in the states would be diminished. It was their object, he said, to keep the King "in tutelage"—to make him a "shadow and a cipher," while they should themselves exercise all authority in the provinces. It is impossible to exaggerate the effect of such suggestions upon the dull and gloomy mind to which they were addressed. It is easy, however, to see that a minister with such views was likely to be as congenial to his master as he was odious to the people. For already, in the beginning of 1562, Granvelle was extremely unpopular. "The Cardinal is hated of all men," wrote Sir Thomas Gresham. The great struggle between him and the leading nobles had already commenced. The people justly identified him with the whole infamous machinery of persecution, which had either originated or warmly made his own. Viglius and Berlaymont were his creatures. With the other members of the state council, according to their solemn statement, already recorded, he did not deign to consult, while he affected to hold them responsible for the measures of the administration. Even the Regent herself complained that the Cardinal took affairs quite out of her hands, and that he decided upon many important matters without her cognizance. She already began to feel herself the puppet which it had been intended she should become; she already felt a diminution of the respectful attachment for the ecclesiastic which had inspired her when she procured his red hat.

Granvelle was, however, most resolute in carrying out the intentions of his master. We have seen how vigorously he had already set himself to the inauguration of the new bishoprics, despite of opposition and obloquy. He was now encouraging or rebuking the inquisitors in their "pious office" throughout all the provinces. Notwithstanding his exertions, however, heresy continued to spread. In the Walloon provinces the infection was most prevalent, while judges and executioners were appalled by the mutinous demonstrations which each successive sacrifice provoked. The victims were cheered on their way to the scaffold. The hymns of Marot were sung in the very faces of the inquisitors. Two ministers, Faveau and Mallart, were particularly conspicuous at this moment at Valenciennes. The governor of the province, Marquis Berghen, was constantly absent, for he hated with his whole soul the system of persecution. For this negligence Granvelle denounced him secretly and perpetually to Philip, "The Marquis says openly," said the Cardinal, "that 'tis not right to shed blood for matters of faith. With such men to aid us, your Majesty can judge how much progress we can make." It was, however, important, in Granvelle's opinion, that these two ministers at Valenciennes should be at once put to death. They were avowed heretics, and they preached to their disciples, although they certainly were not doctors of divinity. Moreover, they were accused, most absurdly, no doubt, of pretending to work miracles. It was said that, in presence of several witnesses, they had undertaken to cast out devils; and they had been apprehended on an accusation of this nature.

> ["Histoire des choses les plus memorables qui se sent passees en la ville et Compte de Valenciennes depuis le commencement des troubles des Pays-Bas sons le regne de Phil. II., jusqu' a l'annee 1621."— MS. (Collect. Gerard).—This is a contemporary manuscript belonging to the Gerard collection in the Royal Library at the Hague. Its author was a citizen of Valenciennes, and a personal witness of most of the events which he describes. He appears to have attained to a great age, as he minutely narrates, from personal observation, many scenes which occurred before 1566, and his work is continued till the year 1621. It is a mere sketch, without much literary merit, but containing many local anecdotes of interest. Its anonymous author was a very sincere Catholic.]

Their offence really consisted in reading the Bible to a few of their friends. Granvelle sent Philibert de Bruxelles to Valenciennes to procure their immediate condemnation and execution. He rebuked the judges and inquisitors, he sent express orders to Marquis Berghen to repair at once to the scene of his duties. The prisoners were condemned in the autumn of 1561. The magistrates were, however, afraid to carry the sentence into effect. Granvelle did not cease to censure them for their pusillanimity, and wrote almost daily letters, accusing the magistrates of being themselves the cause of the tumults by which they were appalled. The popular commotion was, however, not lightly to be braved. Six or seven months long the culprits remained in confinement, while daily and nightly the people crowded the streets, hurling threats and defiance at the authorities, or pressed about the prison windows, encouraging their beloved ministers, and promising to rescue them in case the attempt should be made to fulfil the sentence. At last Granvelle sent down a peremptory order to execute the culprits by fire. On the 27th of April, 1562, Faveau and Mallart were accordingly taken from their jail and carried to the market-place, where arrangements had been made for burning them. Simon Faveau, as the executioner was binding him to the stake, uttered the invocation, "O! Eternal Father!" A woman in the crowd, at the same instant, took off her shoe and threw it at the funeral pile. This was a preconcerted signal. A movement was at once visible in the crowd. Men in great numbers dashed upon the barriers which had been erected in the square around the place of execution. Some seized the fagots, which had been already lighted, and scattered them in every direction; some tore up the pavements; others broke in pieces the barriers. The executioners were prevented from carrying out the sentence, but the guard were enabled, with great celerity and determination, to bring off the culprits and to place them in their dungeon again. The authorities were in doubt and dismay. The inquisitors were for putting the ministers to death in prison, and hurling their heads upon the street. Evening approached while the officials were still pondering. The people who had been chanting the Psalms of David through the town, without having decided what should be their course of action, at last determined to rescue the victims. A vast throng, after much hesitation, accordingly directed their steps to the prison. "You should have seen this vile populace," says an eye-witness, "moving, pausing, recoiling, sweeping forward, swaying to and fro like the waves of the sea when it is agitated by contending winds." The attack was vigorous, the defence was weak—for the authorities had expected no such fierce demonstration, notwithstanding the menacing language which had been so often uttered. The prisoners were rescued, and succeeded in making their escape from the city. The day in which the execution had been thus prevented was called, thenceforward, the "day of the ill-burned," (Journee des mau-brulez). One of the ministers, however, Simon Faveau, not discouraged by this near approach to martyrdom, persisted in his heretical labors, and was a few years afterwards again apprehended. "He was then," says the chronicler, cheerfully, "burned well and finally" in the same place whence he had formerly been rescued. [Valenciennes MS.]

This desperate resistance to tyranny was for a moment successful, because, notwithstanding the murmurs and menaces by which the storm had been preceded, the authorities had not believed the people capable of proceeding to such lengths. Had not the heretics—in the words of Inquisitor Titelmann—allowed themselves, year after year, to be taken and slaughtered like lambs? The consternation of the magistrates was soon succeeded by anger. The government at Brussels was in a frenzy of rage when informed of the occurrence. A bloody vengeance was instantly prepared, to vindicate the insult to the inquisition. On the 29th of April, detachments of Bossu's and of Berghen's "band of ordonnance" were sent into Valenciennes, together with a company of the Duke of Aerschot's regiment. The prisons were instantly filled to overflowing with men and women arrested for actual or suspected participation in the tumult. Orders had been sent down from the capital to make a short process and a sharp execution for all the criminals. On the 16th of May, the slaughter commenced. Some were burned at the stake, some were beheaded: the number of victims was frightful. "Nothing was left undone by the magistrates," says an eyewitness, with great approbation, "which could serve for the correction and amendment of the poor people." It was long before the judges and hangmen rested from their labors. When at last the havoc was complete, it might be supposed that a sufficient vengeance had been taken for the "day of the ill-burned," and an adequate amount of "amendment" provided for the "poor people."

Such scenes as these did not tend to increase the loyalty of the nation, nor the popularity of the government. On Granvelle's head was poured a daily increasing torrent of hatred. He was looked upon in the provinces as the impersonation of that religious oppression which became every moment more intolerable. The King and the Regent escaped much of the odium which belonged to them, because the people chose to bestow all their maledictions upon the Cardinal. There was, however, no great injustice in this embodiment. Granvelle was the government. As the people of that day were extremely reverent to royalty, they vented all their rage upon the minister, while maintaining still a conventional respect for the sovereign. The prelate had already become the constant butt of the "Rhetoric Chambers." These popular clubs for the manufacture of homespun poetry and street farces out of the raw material of public sentiment, occupied the place which has been more effectively filled in succeeding ages, and in free countries by the daily press. Before the invention of that most tremendous weapon, which liberty has ever wielded against tyranny, these humble but influential associations shared with the pulpit the only power which existed of moving the passions or directing the opinions of the people. They were eminently liberal in their tendencies. The authors and the actors of their comedies, poems, and pasquils were mostly artisans or tradesmen, belonging to the class out of which proceeded the early victims, and the later soldiers of the Reformation. Their bold farces and truculent satire had already effected much in spreading among the people a detestation of Church abuses. They were particularly severe upon monastic licentiousness. "These corrupt comedians, called rhetoricians," says the Walloon contemporary already cited, "afforded much amusement to the people." Always some poor little nuns or honest monks were made a part of the farce. It seemed as if the people could take no pleasure except in ridiculing God and the Church. The people, however, persisted in the opinion that the ideas of a monk and of God were not inseparable. Certainly the piety of the early reformers was sufficiently fervent, and had been proved by the steadiness with which they confronted torture and death, but they knew no measure in the ridicule which they heaped upon the men by whom they were daily murdered in droves. The rhetoric comedies were not admirable in an aesthetic point of view, but they were wrathful and sincere. Therefore they cost many thousand lives, but they sowed the seed of resistance to religious tyranny, to spring up one day in a hundredfold harvest. It was natural that the authorities should have long sought to suppress these perambulating dramas. "There was at that tyme," wrote honest Richard Clough to Sir Thomas Gresham, "syche playes (of Reteryke) played thet hath cost many a 1000 man's lyves, for in these plays was the Word of God first opened in thys country. Weche playes were and are forbidden moche more strictly than any of the bookes of Martin Luther."

These rhetoricians were now particularly inflamed against Granvelle. They were personally excited against him, because he had procured the suppression of their religious dramas. "These rhetoricians who make farces and street plays," wrote the Cardinal to Philip, "are particularly angry with me, because two years ago I prevented them from ridiculing the holy Scriptures." Nevertheless, these institutions continued to pursue their opposition to the course of the government. Their uncouth gambols, their awkward but stunning blows rendered daily service to the cause of religious freedom. Upon the newly-appointed bishops they poured out an endless succession of rhymes and rebuses, epigrams, caricatures and extravaganzas. Poems were pasted upon the walls of every house, and passed from hand to hand. Farces were enacted in every street; the odious ecclesiastics figuring as the principal buffoons. These representations gave so much offence, that renewed edicts were issued to suppress them. The prohibition was resisted, and even ridiculed in many provinces, particularly in Holland. The tyranny which was able to drown a nation in blood and tears, was powerless to prevent them from laughing most bitterly at their oppressors. The tanner, Cleon, was never belabored more soundly by the wits of Athens, than the prelate by these Flemish "rhetoricians." With infinitely less Attic salt, but with as much heartiness as Aristophanes could have done, the popular rhymers gave the minister ample opportunity to understand the position which he occupied in the Netherlands. One day a petitioner placed a paper in his hand and vanished. It contained some scurrilous verses upon himself, together with a caricature of his person. In this he was represented as a hen seated upon a pile of eggs, out of which he was hatching a brood of bishops. Some of these were clipping the shell, some thrusting forth an arm, some a leg, while others were running about with mitres on their heads, all bearing whimsical resemblance to various prelates who had been newly-appointed.

Above the Cardinal's head the Devil was represented hovering, with these words issuing from his mouth: "This is my beloved Son, listen to him, my people."

There was another lampoon of a similar nature, which was so well executed, that it especially excited Granvelle's anger. It was a rhymed satire of a general nature, like the rest, but so delicate and so stinging, that the Cardinal ascribed it to his old friend and present enemy, Simon Renard. This man, a Burgundian by birth, and college associate of Granvelle, had been befriended both by himself and his father. Aided by their patronage and his own abilities, he had arrived at distinguished posts; having been Spanish envoy both in France and England, and one of the negotiators of the truce of Vaucelles. He had latterly been disappointed in his ambition to become a councillor of state, and had vowed vengeance upon the Cardinal, to whom he attributed his ill success. He was certainly guilty of much ingratitude, for he had been under early obligations to the man in whose side he now became a perpetual thorn. It must be confessed, on the other hand, that Granvelle repaid the enmity of his old associate with a malevolence equal to his own, and if Renard did not lose his head as well as his political station, it was not for want of sufficient insinuation on the part of the minister. Especially did Granvelle denounce him to "the master" as the perverter of Egmont, while he usually described that nobleman himself, as weak, vain, "a friend of smoke," easily misguided, but in the main well- intentioned and loyal. At the same time, with all these vague commendations, he never omitted to supply the suspicious King with an account of every fact or every rumor to the Count's discredit. In the case of this particular satire, he informed Philip that he could swear it came from the pen of Renard, although, for the sake of deception, the rhetoric comedians had been employed. He described the production as filled with "false, abominable, and infernal things," and as treating not only himself, but the Pope and the whole ecclesiastical order with as much contumely as could be showed in Germany. He then proceeded to insinuate, in the subtle manner which was peculiarly his own, that Egmont was a party to the publication of the pasquil. Renard visited at that house, he said, and was received there on a much more intimate footing than was becoming. Eight days before the satire was circulated, there had been a conversation in Egmont's house, of a nature exactly similar to the substance of the pamphlet. The man, in whose hands it was first seen, continued Granvelle, was a sword cutler, a godson of the Count. This person said that he had torn it from the gate of the city hall, but God grant, prayed the Cardinal, that it was not he who had first posted it up there. 'Tis said that Egmont and Mansfeld, he added, have sent many times to the cutler to procure copies of the satire, all which augments the suspicion against them.

With the nobles he was on no better terms than with the people. The great seigniors, Orange, Egmont, Horn, and others, openly avowed their hostility to him, and had already given their reasons to the King. Mansfeld and his son at that time were both with the opposition. Aerschot and Aremberg kept aloof from the league which was forming against the prelate, but had small sympathy for his person. Even Berlaymont began to listen to overtures from the leading nobles, who, among other inducements, promised to supply his children with bishoprics. There were none truly faithful and submissive to the Cardinal but such men as the Prevot Morillon, who had received much advancement from him.

This distinguished pluralist was popularly called "double A, B, C," to indicate that he had twice as many benefices as there were letters in the alphabet. He had, however, no objection to more, and was faithful to the dispensing power. The same course was pursued by Secretary Bave, Esquire Bordey, and other expectants and dependents. Viglius, always remarkable for his pusillanimity, was at this period already anxious to retire. The erudite and opulent Frisian preferred a less tempestuous career. He was in favor of the edicts, but he trembled at the uproar which their literal execution was daily exciting, for he knew the temper of his countrymen. On the other hand, he was too sagacious not to know the inevitable consequence of opposition to the will of Philip. He was therefore most eager to escape the dilemma. He was a scholar, and could find more agreeable employment among his books. He had accumulated vast wealth, and was desirous to retain it as long as possible. He had a learned head and was anxious to keep it upon his shoulders. These simple objects could be better attained in a life of privacy. The post of president of the privy council and member of the "Consulta" was a dangerous one. He knew that the King was sincere in his purposes. He foresaw that the people would one day be terribly in earnest. Of ancient Frisian blood himself, he knew that the, spirit of the ancient Batavians and Frisians had not wholly deserted their descendants. He knew that they were not easily roused, that they were patient, but that they would strike at last and would endure. He urgently solicited the King to release him, and pleaded his infirmities of body in excuse. Philip, however, would not listen to his retirement, and made use of the most convincing arguments to induce him to remain. Four hundred and fifty annual florins, secured by good reclaimed swamps in Friesland, two thousand more in hand, with a promise of still larger emoluments when the King should come to the Netherlands, were reasons which the learned doctor honestly confessed himself unable to resist. Fortified by these arguments, he remained at his post, continued the avowed friend and adherent of Granvelle, and sustained with magnanimity the invectives of nobles and people. To do him justice, he did what he could to conciliate antagonists and to compromise principles. If it had ever been possible to find the exact path between right and wrong, the President would have found it, and walked in it with respectability and complacency.

In the council, however, the Cardinal continued to carry it with a high hand; turning his back on Orange and Egmont, and retiring with the Duchess and President to consult, after every session. Proud and important personages, like the Prince and Count, could ill brook such insolence; moreover, they suspected the Cardinal of prejudicing the mind of their sovereign against them. A report was very current, and obtained almost universal belief, that Granvelle had expressly advised his Majesty to take off the heads of at least half a dozen of the principal nobles in the land. This was an error; "These two seigniors," wrote the Cardinal to Philip, "have been informed that I have written to your Majesty, that you will never be master of these provinces without taking off at least half a dozen heads, and that because it would be difficult, on account of the probable tumults which such a course would occasion, to do it here, your Majesty means to call them to Spain and do it there. Your Majesty can judge whether such a thing has ever entered my thoughts. I have laughed at it as a ridiculous invention. This gross forgery is one of Renard's." The Cardinal further stated to his Majesty that he had been informed by these same nobles that the Duke of Alva, when a hostage for the treaty of Cateau Cambresis, had negotiated an alliance between the crowns of France and Spain for the extirpation of heresy by the sword. He added, that he intended to deal with the nobles with all gentleness, and that he should do his best to please them. The only thing which he could not yield was the authority of his Majesty; to sustain that, he would sacrifice his life, if necessary. At the same time Granvelle carefully impressed upon the King the necessity of contradicting the report alluded to, a request which he took care should also be made through the Regent in person. He had already, both in his own person and in that of the Duchess, begged for a formal denial, on the King's part, that there was any intention of introducing the Spanish inquisition into the Netherlands, and that the Cardinal had counselled, originally, the bishoprics. Thus instructed, the King accordingly wrote to Margaret of Parma to furnish the required contradictions. In so doing, he made a pithy remark. "The Cardinal had not counselled the cutting off the half a dozen heads," said the monarch, "but perhaps it would not be so bad to do it!" Time was to show whether Philip was likely to profit by the hint conveyed in the Cardinal's disclaimer, and whether the factor "half dozen" were to be used or not as a simple multiplier in the terrible account preparing.

The contradictions, however sincere, were not believed by the persons most interested. Nearly all the nobles continued to regard the Cardinal with suspicion and aversion. Many of the ruder and more reckless class vied with the rhetoricians and popular caricaturists in the practical jests which they played off almost daily against the common foe. Especially Count Brederode, "a madman, if there ever were one," as a contemporary expressed himself, was most untiring in his efforts to make Granvelle ridiculous. He went almost nightly to masquerades, dressed as a cardinal or a monk; and as he was rarely known to be sober on these or any other occasions, the wildness of his demonstrations may easily be imagined. He was seconded on all these occasions by his cousin Robert de la Marck, Seigneur de Lumey, a worthy descendant of the famous "Wild Boar of Ardennes;" a man brave to temerity, but utterly depraved, licentious, and sanguinary. These two men, both to be widely notorious, from their prominence in many of the most striking scenes by which the great revolt was ushered in, had vowed the most determined animosity to the Cardinal, which was manifested in the reckless, buffooning way which belonged to their characters. Besides the ecclesiastical costumes in which they always attired themselves at their frequent festivities, they also wore fog-tails in their hats instead of plumes. They decked their servants also with the same ornaments; openly stating, that by these symbols they meant to signify that the old fox Granvelle, and his cubs, Viglius, Berlaymont, and the rest, should soon be hunted down by them, and the brush placed in their hats as a trophy.

Moreover, there is no doubt that frequent threats of personal violence were made against the Cardinal. Granvelle informed the King that his life was continually menaced by, the nobles, but that he feared them little, "for he believed them too prudent to attempt any thing of the kind." There is no doubt, when his position with regard to the upper and lower classes in the country is considered, that there was enough to alarm a timid man; but Granvelle was constitutionally brave. He was accused of wearing a secret shirt of mail, of living in perpetual trepidation, of having gone on his knees to Egmont and Orange, of having sent Richardot, Bishop of Arras, to intercede for him in the same humiliating manner with Egmont. All these stories were fables. Bold as he was arrogant, he affected at this time to look down with a forgiving contempt on the animosity of the nobles. He passed much of his time alone, writing his eternal dispatches to the King. He had a country- house, called La Fontaine, surrounded by beautiful gardens, a little way outside the gates of Brussels, where he generally resided, and whence, notwithstanding the remonstrances of his friends, he often returned to town, after sunset, alone, or with but a few attendants. He avowed that he feared no attempts at assassination, for, if the seigniors took his life, they would destroy the best friend they ever had. This villa, where most of his plans were matured and his state papers drawn up, was called by the people, in derision of his supposed ancestry, "The Smithy." Here, as they believed, was the anvil upon which the chains of their slavery were forging; here, mostly deserted by those who had been his earlier, associates, he assumed a philosophical demeanor which exasperated, without deceiving his adversaries. Over the great gate of his house he had placed the marble statue of a female. It held an empty wine-cup in one hand, and an urn of flowing water in the other. The single word "Durate" was engraved upon the pedestal. By the motto, which was his habitual device, he was supposed, in this application, to signify that his power would outlast that of the nobles, and that perennial and pure as living water, it would flow tranquilly on, long after the wine of their life had been drunk to the lees. The fiery extravagance of his adversaries, and the calm and limpid moderation of his own character, thus symbolized, were supposed to convey a moral lesson to the world. The hieroglyphics, thus interpreted, were not relished by the nobles—all avoided his society, and declined his invitations. He consoled himself with the company of the lesser gentry, —a class which he now began to patronize, and which he urgently recommended to the favor of the King,—hinting that military and civil offices bestowed upon their inferiors would be a means of lowering the pride of the grandees. He also affected to surround himself with even humbler individuals. "It makes me laugh," he wrote to Philip, "to see the great seigniors absenting themselves from my dinners; nevertheless, I can always get plenty of guests at my table, gentlemen and councillors. I sometimes invite even citizens, in order to gain their good will."

The Regent was well aware of the anger excited in the breasts of the leading nobles by the cool manner in which they had been thrust out of their share in the administration of affairs. She defended herself with acrimony in her letters to the King, although a defence was hardly needed in that quarter for implicit obedience to the royal commands. She confessed her unwillingness to consult with her enemies.

She avowed her determination to conceal the secrets of the government from those who were capable of abusing her confidence. She represented that there were members of the council who would willingly take advantage of the trepidation which she really felt, and which she should exhibit if she expressed herself without reserve before them. For this reason she confined herself, as Philip had always intended, exclusively to the Consulta. It was not difficult to recognize the hand which wrote the letter thus signed by Margaret of Parma.

Both nobles and people were at this moment irritated by another circumstance. The civil war having again broken out in France, Philip, according to the promise made by him to Catharine de Medici, when he took her daughter in marriage, was called upon to assist the Catholic party with auxiliaries. He sent three thousand infantry, accordingly, which he had levied in Italy, as many more collected in Spain, and gave immediate orders that the Duchess of Parma should despatch at least two thousand cavalry, from the Netherlands. Great was the indignation in the council when the commands were produced. Sore was the dismay of Margaret. It was impossible to obey the King. The idea of sending the famous mounted gendarmerie of the provinces to fight against the French Huguenots could not be tolerated for an instant. The "bands of ordonnance" were very few in number, and were to guard the frontier. They were purely for domestic purposes. It formed no part of their duty to go upon crusades in foreign lands; still less to take a share in a religious quarrel, and least of all to assist a monarch against a nation. These views were so cogently presented to the Duchess in council, that she saw the impossibility of complying with her brother's commands. She wrote to Philip to that effect. Meantime, another letter arrived out of Spain, chiding her delay, and impatiently calling upon her to furnish the required cavalry at once. The Duchess was in a dilemma. She feared to provoke another storm in the council, for there was already sufficient wrangling there upon domestic subjects. She knew it was impossible to obtain the consent, even of Berlaymont and Viglius, to such an odious measure as the one proposed. She was, however, in great trepidation at the peremptory tone of the King's despatch. Under the advice of Granvelle, she had recourse to a trick. A private and confidential letter of Philip was read to the council, but with alterations suggested and interpolated by the Cardinal. The King was represented as being furious at the delay, but as willing that a sum of money should be furnished instead of the cavalry, as originally required. This compromise, after considerable opposition, was accepted. The Duchess wrote to Philip, explaining and apologizing for the transaction. The King received the substitution with as good a grace as could have been expected, and sent fifteen hundred troopers from Spain to his Medicean mother-in-law, drawing upon the Duchess of Parma for the money to pay their expenses. Thus was the industry of the Netherlands taxed that the French might be persecuted by their own monarch.

The Regent had been forbidden, by her brother, to convoke the states-general; a body which the Prince of Orange, sustained by Berghen, Montigny, and other nobles, was desirous of having assembled. It may be easily understood that Granvelle would take the best care that the royal prohibition should be enforced. The Duchess, however, who, as already hinted, was beginning to feel somewhat uncomfortable under the Cardinal's dominion, was desirous of consulting some larger council than that with which she held her daily deliberations. A meeting of the Knights of the Fleece was accordingly summoned. They assembled in Brussels, in the month of May, 1562. The learned Viglius addressed them in a long and eloquent speech, in which he discussed the troubled and dangerous condition of the provinces, alluded to some of its causes, and suggested various remedies. It may be easily conceived, however, that the inquisition was not stated among the causes, nor its suppression included among the remedies. A discourse, in which the fundamental topic was thus conscientiously omitted, was not likely, with all its concinnities, to make much impression upon the disaffected knights, or to exert a soothing influence upon the people. The orator was, however, delighted with his own performance. He informs us, moreover, that the Duchess was equally charmed, and that she protested she had never in her whole life heard any thing more "delicate, more suitable, or more eloquent." The Prince of Orange, however, did not sympathize with her admiration. The President's elegant periods produced but little effect upon his mind. The meeting adjourned, after a few additional words from the Duchess, in which she begged the knights to ponder well the causes of the increasing discontent, and to meet her again, prepared to announce what, in their opinion, would be the course best adapted to maintain the honor of the King, the safety of the provinces, and the glory of God.

Soon after the separation of the assembly, the Prince of Orange issued invitations to most of the knights, to meet at his house for the purpose of private deliberation. The President and Cardinal were not included in these invitations. The meeting was, in fact, what we should call a caucus, rather than a general gathering. Nevertheless, there were many of the government party present—men who differed from the Prince, and were inclined to support Granvelle. The meeting was a stormy one. Two subjects were discussed. The first was the proposition of the Duchess, to investigate the general causes of the popular dissatisfaction; the second was an inquiry how it could be rendered practicable to discuss political matters in future—a proceeding now impossible, in consequence of the perverseness and arrogance of certain functionaries, and one which, whenever attempted, always led to the same inevitable result. This direct assault upon the Cardinal produced a furious debate. His enemies were delighted with the opportunity of venting their long- suppressed spleen. They indulged in savage invectives against the man whom they so sincerely hated. His adherents, on the other hand—Bossu, Berlaymont, Courieres—were as warm in his defence. They replied by indignant denials of the charge against him, and by bitter insinuations against the Prince of Orange. They charged him with nourishing the desire of being appointed governor of Brabant, an office considered inseparable from the general stadholderate of all the provinces. They protested for themselves that they were actuated by no ambitious designs —that they were satisfied with their own position, and not inspired by jealousy of personages more powerful than themselves. It is obvious that such charges and recriminations could excite no healing result, and that the lines between Cardinalists and their opponents would be defined in consequence more sharply than ever. The adjourned meeting of the Chevaliers of the Fleece took place a few days afterwards. The Duchess exerted herself as much as possible to reconcile the contending factions, without being able, however, to apply the only remedy which could be effective. The man who was already fast becoming the great statesman of the country knew that the evil was beyond healing, unless by a change of purpose on the part of the government. The Regent, on the other hand, who it must be confessed never exhibited any remarkable proof of intellectual ability during the period of her residence in the Netherlands, was often inspired by a feeble and indefinite hope that the matter might be arranged by a compromise between the views of conflicting parties. Unfortunately the inquisition was not a fit subject for a compromise.

Nothing of radical importance was accomplished by the Assembly of the Fleece. It was decided that an application should be made to the different states for a giant of money, and that, furthermore, a special envoy should be despatched to Spain. It was supposed by the Duchess and her advisers that more satisfactory information concerning the provinces could be conveyed to Philip by word of mouth than by the most elaborate epistles. The meeting was dissolved after these two measures had been agreed upon. Doctor Viglius, upon whom devolved the duty of making the report and petition to the states, proceeded to draw up the necessary application. This he did with his customary elegance, and, as usual, very much to his own satisfaction. On returning to his house, however, after having discharged this duty, he was very much troubled at finding that a large mulberry-tree; which stood in his garden, had been torn up by the roots in a violent hurricane. The disaster was considered ominous by the President, and he was accordingly less surprised than mortified when he found, subsequently, that his demand upon the orders had remained as fruitless as his ruined tree. The tempest which had swept his garden he considered typical of the storm which was soon to rage through the land, and he felt increased anxiety to reach a haven while it was yet comparatively calm.

The estates rejected the request for supplies, on various grounds; among others, that the civil war was drawing to a conclusion in France, and that less danger was to be apprehended from that source than had lately been the case. Thus, the "cup of bitterness," of which Granvelle had already complained; was again commended to his lips, and there was more reason than ever for the government to regret that the national representatives had contracted the habit of meddling with financial matters.

Florence de Montmorency, Seigneur de Montigny, was selected by the Regent for the mission which had been decided upon for Spain. This gentleman was brother to Count Horn, but possessed of higher talents and a more amiable character than those of the Admiral. He was a warm friend of Orange, and a bitter enemy to Granvelle. He was a sincere Catholic, but a determined foe to the inquisition. His brother had declined to act as envoy. This refusal can excite but little surprise, when Philip's wrath at their parting interview is recalled, and when it is also remembered that the new mission would necessarily lay bare fresh complaints against the Cardinal, still more extensive than those which had produced the former explosion of royal indignation. Montigny, likewise, would have preferred to remain at home, but he was overruled. It had been written in his destiny that he should go twice into the angry lion's den, and that he should come forth once, alive.

Thus it has been shown that there was an open, avowed hostility on the part of the grand seignors and most of the lesser nobility to the Cardinal and his measures. The people fully and enthusiastically sustained the Prince of Orange in his course. There was nothing underhand in the opposition made to the government. The Netherlands did not constitute an absolute monarchy. They did not even constitute a monarchy. There was no king in the provinces. Philip was King of Spain, Naples, Jerusalem, but he was only Duke of Brabant, Count of Flanders, Lord of Friesland, hereditary chief, in short, under various titles, of seventeen states, each one of which, although not republican, possessed constitutions as sacred as, and much more ancient than, the Crown. The resistance to the absolutism of Granvelle and Philip was, therefore, logical, legal, constitutional. It was no cabal, no secret league, as the Cardinal had the effrontery to term it, but a legitimate exercise of powers which belonged of old to those who wielded them, and which only an unrighteous innovation could destroy.

Granvelle's course was secret and subtle. During the whole course of the proceedings which have just been described, he was; in daily confidential correspondence with the King, besides being the actual author of the multitudinous despatches which were sent with the signature of the Duchess. He openly asserted his right to monopolize all the powers of the Government; he did his utmost to force upon the reluctant and almost rebellious people the odious measures which the King had resolved upon, while in his secret letters he uniformly represented the nobles who opposed him, as being influenced, not by an honest hatred of oppression and attachment to ancient rights, but by resentment, and jealousy of their own importance. He assumed, in his letters to his master, that the absolutism already existed of right and in fact, which it was the intention of Philip to establish. While he was depriving the nobles, the states and the nation of their privileges, and even of their natural rights (a slender heritage in those days), he assured the King that there was an evident determination to reduce his authority to a cipher.

The estates, he wrote, had usurped the whole administration of the finances, and had farmed it out to Antony Van Stralen and others, who were making enormous profits in the business. "The seignors," he said, "declare at their dinner parties that I wish to make them subject to the absolute despotism of your Majesty. In point of fact, however, they really exercise a great deal more power than the governors of particular provinces ever did before; and it lacks but little that Madame and your Majesty should become mere ciphers, while the grandees monopolize the whole power. This," he continued, "is the principal motive of their opposition to the new bishoprics. They were angry that your Majesty should have dared to solicit such an arrangement at Rome, without, first obtaining their consent. They wish to reduce your Majesty's authority to so low a point that you can do nothing unless they desire it. Their object is the destruction of the royal authority and of the administration of justice, in order to avoid the payment of their debts; telling their creditors constantly that they, have spent their all in your Majesty's service, and that they have never received recompence or salary. This they do to make your Majesty odious."

As a matter of course, he attributed the resistance on the part of the great nobles, every man of whom was Catholic, to base motives. They were mere demagogues, who refused to burn their fellow-creatures, not from any natural repugnance to the task, but in order to gain favor with the populace. "This talk about the inquisition," said he, "is all a pretext. 'Tis only to throw dust in the eyes of the vulgar, and to persuade them into tumultuous demonstrations, while the real reason is, that they choose that your Majesty should do nothing without their permission, and through their hands."

He assumed sometimes, however, a tone of indulgence toward the seignors —who formed the main topics of his letters—an affectation which might, perhaps, have offended them almost as much as more open and sincere denunciation. He could forgive offences against himself. It was for Philip to decide as to their merits or crimes so far as the Crown was concerned. His language often was befitting a wise man who was speaking of very little children. "Assonleville has told me, as coming from Egmont," he wrote, "that many of the nobles are dissatisfied with me; hearing from Spain that I am endeavoring to prejudice your Majesty against them." Certainly the tone of the Cardinal's daily letters would have justified such suspicion, could the nobles have seen them. Granvelle begged the King, however, to disabuse them upon this point. "Would to God," said he, piously, "that they all would decide to sustain the authority of your Majesty, and to procure such measures as tend to the service of God and the security of the states. May I cease to exist if I do not desire to render good service to the very least of these gentlemen. Your Majesty knows that, when they do any thing for the benefit of your service, I am never silent. Nevertheless, thus they are constituted. I hope, however, that this flurry will blow over, and that when your Majesty comes they will all be found to deserve rewards of merit."

Of Egmont, especially, he often spoke in terms of vague, but somewhat condescending commendation. He never manifested resentment in his letters, although, as already stated, the Count had occasionally indulged, not only in words, but in deeds of extreme violence against him. But the Cardinal was too forgiving a Christian, or too keen a politician not to pass by such offences, so long as there was a chance of so great a noble's remaining or becoming his friend. He, accordingly, described him, in general, as a man whose principles, in the main, were good, but who was easily led by his own vanity and the perverse counsels of others. He represented him as having been originally a warm supporter of the new bishoprics, and as having expressed satisfaction that two of them, those of Bruges and Ypres, should have been within his own stadholderate. He regretted, however; to inform the King that the Count was latterly growing lukewarm, perhaps from fear of finding himself separated from the other nobles. On the whole, he was tractable enough, said the Cardinal, if he were not easily persuaded by the vile; but one day, perhaps, he might open his eyes again. Notwithstanding these vague expressions of approbation, which Granvelle permitted himself in his letters to Philip, he never failed to transmit to the monarch every fact, every rumor, every inuendo which might prejudice the royal mind against that nobleman or against any of the noblemen, whose characters he at the same time protested he was most unwilling to injure.

It is true that he dealt mainly by insinuation, while he was apt to conclude his statements with disclaimers upon his own part, and with hopes of improvement in the conduct of the seignors. At this particular point of time he furnished Philip with a long and most circumstantial account of a treasonable correspondence which was thought to be going on between the leading nobles and the future emperor, Maximilian. The narrative was a good specimen of the masterly style of inuendo in which the Cardinal excelled, and by which he was often enabled to convince his master of the truth of certain statements while affecting to discredit them. He had heard a story, he said, which he felt bound to communicate to his Majesty, although he did not himself implicitly believe it. He felt himself the more bound to speak upon the subject because it tallied exactly with intelligence which he had received from another source. The story was that one of these seigniors (the Cardinal did not know which, for he had not yet thought proper to investigate the matter) had said that rather than consent that the King should act in this matter of the bishoprics against the privileges of Brabant, the nobles would elect for their sovereign some other prince of the blood. This, said the Cardinal, was perhaps a fantasy rather than an actual determination. Count Egmont, to be sure, he said, was constantly exchanging letters with the King of Bohemia (Maximilian), and it was supposed, therefore, that he was the prince of the blood who was to be elected to govern the provinces. It was determined that he should be chosen King of the Romans, by fair means or by force, that he should assemble an army to attack the Netherlands, that a corresponding movement should be made within the states, and that the people should be made to rise, by giving them the reins in the matter of religion. The Cardinal, after recounting all the particulars of this fiction with great minuteness, added, with apparent frankness, that the correspondence between Egmont and Maximilian did not astonish him, because there had been much intimacy between them in the time of the late Emperor. He did not feel convinced, therefore, from the frequency of the letters exchanged, that there was a scheme to raise an army to attack the provinces and to have him elected by force. On the contrary, Maximilian could never accomplish such a scheme without the assistance of his imperial father the Emperor, whom Granvelle was convinced would rather die than be mixed up with such villany against Philip. Moreover, unless the people should become still more corrupted by the bad counsels constantly given them, the Cardinal did not believe that any of the great nobles had the power to dispose in this way of the provinces at their pleasure. Therefore, he concluded that the story was to be rejected as improbable, although it had come to him directly from the house of the said Count Egmont. It is remarkable that, at the commencement of his narrative, the Cardinal had expressed his ignorance of the name of the seignior who was hatching all this treason, while at the end of it he gave a local habitation to the plot in the palace of Egmont. It is also quite characteristic that he should add that, after all, he considered that nobleman one of the most honest of all, if appearances did not deceive.

It may be supposed, however, that all these details of a plot which was quite imaginary, were likely to produce more effect upon a mind so narrow and so suspicious as that of Philip, than could the vague assertions of the Cardinal, that in spite of all, he would dare be sworn that he thought the Count honest, and that men should be what they seemed.

Notwithstanding the conspiracy, which, according to Granvelle's letters, had been formed against him, notwithstanding that his life was daily threatened, he did not advise the King at this period to avenge him by any public explosion of wrath. He remembered, he piously observed, that vengeance belonged to God, and that He would repay. Therefore he passed over insults meekly, because that comported best with his Majesty's service. Therefore, too, he instructed Philip to make no demonstration at that time, in order not to damage his own affairs. He advised him to dissemble, and to pretend not to know what was going on in the provinces. Knowing that his master looked to him daily for instructions, always obeyed them with entire docility, and, in fact, could not move a step in Netherland matters without them, he proceeded to dictate to him the terms in which he was to write to the nobles, and especially laid down rules for his guidance in his coming interviews with the Seigneur de Montigny. Philip, whose only talent consisted in the capacity to learn such lessons with laborious effort, was at this juncture particularly in need of tuition. The Cardinal instructed him, accordingly, that he was to disabuse all men of the impression that the Spanish inquisition was to be introduced into the provinces. He was to write to the seigniors, promising to pay them their arrears of salary; he was to exhort them to do all in their power for the advancement of religion and maintenance of the royal authority; and he was to suggest to them that, by his answer to the Antwerp deputation, it was proved that there was no intention of establishing the inquisition of Spain, under pretext of the new bishoprics.

The King was, furthermore, to signify his desire that all the nobles should exert themselves to efface this false impression from the popular mind. He was also to express himself to the same effect concerning the Spanish inquisition, the bishoprics, and the religious question, in the public letters to Madame de Parma, which were to be read in full council. The Cardinal also renewed his instructions to the King as to the manner in which the Antwerp deputies were to be answered, by giving them, namely, assurances that to transplant the Spanish inquisition into the provinces would be as hopeless as to attempt its establishment in Naples. He renewed his desire that Philip should contradict the story about the half dozen heads, and he especially directed him to inform Montigny that Berghen had known of the new bishoprics before the Cardinal. This, urged Granvelle, was particularly necessary, because the seigniors were irritated that so important a matter should have been decided upon without their advice, and because the Marquis Berghen was now the "cock of the opposition."

At about the same time, it was decided by Granvelle and the Regent, in conjunction with the King, to sow distrust and jealousy among the nobles, by giving greater "mercedes" to some than to others, although large sums were really due to all. In particular, the attempt was made in this paltry manner, to humiliate William of Orange. A considerable sum was paid to Egmont, and a trifling one to the Prince, in consideration of their large claims upon the treasury. Moreover the Duke of Aerschot was selected as envoy to the Frankfort Diet, where the King of the Romans was to be elected, with the express intention, as Margaret wrote to Philip, of creating divisions among the nobles, as he had suggested. The Duchess at the same time informed her brother that, according to, Berlaymont, the Prince of Orange was revolving some great design, prejudicial to his Majesty's service.

Philip, who already began to suspect that a man who thought so much must be dangerous, was eager to find out the scheme over which William the Silent was supposed to be brooding, and wrote for fresh intelligence to the Duchess.

Neither Margaret nor the Cardinal, however, could discover any thing against the Prince—who, meantime, although disappointed of the mission to Frankfort, had gone to that city in his private capacity—saving that he had been heard to say, "one day we shall be the stronger." Granvelle and Madame de Parma both communicated this report upon the same day, but this was all that they were able to discover of the latent plot.

In the autumn of this year (1562) Montigny made his visit to Spain, as confidential envoy from the Regent. The King being fully prepared as to the manner in which he was to deal with him, received the ambassador with great cordiality. He informed him in the course of their interviews, that Granvelle had never attempted to create prejudice against the nobles, that he was incapable of the malice attributed to him, and that even were it otherwise, his evil representations against other public servants would produce no effect. The King furthermore protested that he had no intention of introducing the Spanish inquisition into the Netherlands, and that the new bishops were not intended as agents for such a design, but had been appointed solely with a view of smoothing religious difficulties in the provinces, and of leading his people back into the fold of the faithful. He added, that as long ago as his visit to England for the purpose of espousing Queen Mary, he had entertained the project of the new episcopates, as the Marquis Berghen, with whom he had conversed freely upon the subject, could bear witness. With regard to the connexion of Granvelle with the scheme, he assured Montigny that the Cardinal had not been previously consulted, but had first learned the plan after the mission of Sonnius.

Such was the purport of the King's communications to the envoy, as appears from memoranda in the royal handwriting and from the correspondence of Margaret of Parma. Philip's exactness in conforming to his instructions is sufficiently apparent, on comparing his statements with the letters previously received from the omnipresent Cardinal. Beyond the limits of those directions the King hardly hazarded a syllable. He was merely the plenipotentiary of the Cardinal, as Montigny was of the Regent. So long as Granvelle's power lasted, he was absolute and infallible. Such, then, was the amount of satisfaction derived from the mission of Montigny. There was to be no diminution of the religious persecution, but the people were assured upon royal authority, that the inquisition, by which they were daily burned and beheaded, could not be logically denominated the Spanish inquisition. In addition to the comfort, whatever it might be, which the nation could derive from this statement, they were also consoled with the information that Granvelle was not the inventor of the bishoprics. Although he had violently supported the measure as soon as published, secretly denouncing as traitors and demagogues, all those who lifted their voices against it, although he was the originator of the renewed edicts, although he took, daily, personal pains that this Netherland inquisition, "more pitiless than the Spanish," should be enforced in its rigor, and although he, at the last, opposed the slightest mitigation of its horrors, he was to be represented to the nobles and the people as a man of mild and unprejudiced character, incapable of injuring even his enemies. "I will deal with the seigniors most blandly," the Cardinal had written to Philip, "and will do them pleasure, even if they do not wish it, for the sake of God and your Majesty." It was in this light, accordingly, that Philip drew the picture of his favorite minister to the envoy. Montigny, although somewhat influenced by the King's hypocritical assurances of the, benignity with which he regarded the Netherlands, was, nevertheless, not to be deceived by this flattering portraiture of a man whom he knew so well and detested so cordially as he did Granvelle. Solicited by the King, at their parting interview, to express his candid opinion as to the causes of the dissatisfaction in the provinces, Montigny very frankly and most imprudently gave vent to his private animosity towards the Cardinal. He spoke of his licentiousness, greediness, ostentation, despotism, and assured the monarch that nearly all the inhabitants of the Netherlands entertained the same opinion concerning him. He then dilated upon the general horror inspired by the inquisition and the great repugnance felt to the establishment of the new episcopates. These three evils, Granvelle, the inquisition, and the bishoprics, he maintained were the real and sufficient causes of the increasing popular discontent. Time was to reveal whether the open-hearted envoy was to escape punishment for his frankness, and whether vengeance for these crimes against Granvelle and Philip were to be left wholly, as the Cardinal had lately suggested, in the hands of the Lord.

Montigny returned late in December. His report concerning the results of his mission was made in the state council, and was received with great indignation. The professions of benevolent intentions on the part of the sovereign made no impression on the mind of Orange, who was already in the habit of receiving secret information from Spain with regard to the intentions of the government. He knew very well that the plot revealed to him by Henry the Second in the wood of Vincennes was still the royal program, so far as the Spanish monarch was concerned. Moreover, his anger was heightened by information received from Montigny that the names of Orange, Egmont and their adherents, were cited to him as he passed through France as the avowed defenders of the Huguenots, in politics and religion. The Prince, who was still a sincere Catholic, while he hated the persecutions of the inquisition, was furious at the statement. A violent scene occurred in the council. Orange openly denounced the report as a new slander of Granvelle, while Margaret defended the Cardinal and denied the accusation, but at the same time endeavored with the utmost earnestness to reconcile the conflicting parties.

It had now become certain, however, that the government could no longer be continued on its present footing. Either Granvelle or the seigniors must succumb. The Prince of Orange was resolved that the Cardinal should fall or that he would himself withdraw from all participation in the affairs of government. In this decision he was sustained by Egmont, Horn, Montigny, Berghen, and the other leading nobles.